America Was Beautiful

BARRE PUBLISHERS
BARRE, MASSACHUSETTS

America Was Beautiful

Edited by	ALICE WATSON
Introduction by	ARTHUR A. HOUGHTON, JR.
Designed by	JAMES HOUSTON

Copyright © 1969 by Barre Publishers
Library of Congress Catalog Card No. 70-87003
ISBN 8271-7210-9
Printing by The Meriden Gravure Company
Binding by The Sendor Bindery
Manufactured in The United States of America
All rights reserved
Second printing January 1972

FRONT COVER: *The Highlands of the Neversink*
BACK COVER: *The Housatonic*
END PAPERS: *On the Beach, Newport*
HALF TITLE: *Rainbow Falls, Watkins Glen*
TITLE PAGE: *Above the Natural Bridge*
LIST OF ENGRAVINGS: *Mount Mansfield*
PAGE 6: *Connecticut River Valley*
INTRODUCTION: *Mackinac*

LIST OF ENGRAVINGS

PREFACE

This book is a collection of wood and steel engravings originally published in 1872-74 in two heavy volumes entitled *Picturesque America*. Published by D. Appleton & Co., New York, Volume I, containing 568 pages, appeared in 1872, and Volume II, with 576 pages, appeared in 1874. Each volume (10 x 13 inches) was bound in brown leather. The production of the books was conceived by George S. Appleton and Oliver B. Bunce, both considered men of taste. It was one of the greatest publishing ventures undertaken to that time in the young United States and its very cost, reputedly over $100,000, indicates the seriousness of the publishers and their confidence that the book would evoke great public appeal. The large organization of the publication was handled by Oliver B. Bunce, and the introduction was written and proof sheets read by William Cullen Bryant. The project required the talents of 28 writers and more than 30 artists and engravers.

Although the selection of engravings chosen for *America Was Beautiful* can show only a few of the choicest places of natural beauty and historical interest, these nostalgic images reflect the magnitude of the Republic spanning the whole glor-ious continent. Each subject is an inspiration for the artist, a theme for the poet, a discovery for the geologist, and an exciting clue for the historian. The original titles used in *Picturesque America* have been retained, but during the past years some of these names have changed. The spelling has been modernized. Most of the descriptions accompanying the engravings use the very words that expressed the feelings of America a century ago. It is somewhat surprising to hear of a river with "an evil reputation for its sadness and loneliness," and some of our countrymen referred to as "denizens of the swamps." Where now are "the panthers and the grand black war eagles" of the Adirondacks, and what has happened to the "half savage outlandish fellows" who were rivermen on the Wisconsin? In essence, the purpose of this book is to try to reveal something of the romantic mood and character of late 19th-century America and to remind us that our history is still around us, a part of the boundless gift of our great heritage.

Alice Watson

INTRODUCTION

A century ago a small task force of artists and writers were commissioned to travel into every corner of this country in search of the spectacular and the beautiful, in search of picturesque America. Sparked by the imagination of William Cullen Bryant and armed only with easels and pens, these intrepid men of talent took to their separate ways. Some toiled up the highest mountains of the Adirondacks, others trekked into the savannas and bayous of the Gulf coast, still others journeyed across the Indian territories of the open West.

To reach their destinations, the artists and writers traveled on horseback and boarded trains drawn by puffing locomotives on rails that had at last managed to span the continent. Sometimes they ran the rapids in frail canoes or passed leisurely down the broad Mississippi in paddle-wheel steamers called "floating palaces." They recorded the glory of America which hitherto had been known to most of the world only through academic surveys and geological reports.

They visited many towns and small cities still bearing Indian names. As if by magic, many of these had changed from remote trading posts and trappers' villages into gentle communities with well planned streets shaded by spreading trees. Church spires rose above the avenues of neat white houses, and the cities were filled with new noises—the whirring and tapping of a thousand growing industries. It was the dawn of high hope in America, an exciting time for every man, a time to discover the length and breadth and endless possibilities of the land. Indeed, America was beautiful.

It was an age of adventure, hard work, and delicious leisure. It was an age of invention and political passion. For many it was still a rural period that had existed before the fences forced the buffalo from the central plains. The Union had only thirty-seven states. The geysers of Yellowstone still belonged in the territories, and far-off Alaska still belonged to the Russian tsar.

Since then, a century of rapid technological development has followed, bringing tremendous developments in almost every field. In the rush to achieve new goals, neglect of conservation has left our land badly scarred. The early settlers in America had to fight against the forest and feed on its fish and wild game as they cleared the land to make farms and build the towns. Now the wild game has disappeared and the towns have grown into metropolises linked by wide-laned highways. A thousand houses, shops, and factories have sprung up along these roads and merged one city into another at a rate that staggers the imagination. One river mentioned in this book now carries so much chemical waste that the river itself has become a serious fire hazard that sometimes bursts into flame, burning its banks and melting its bridges.

Fortunately, we are at last becoming alarmed at our own neglect. We have the technical ability to clean our lakes and rivers, we know how to sweep away the rusting junk yards that mar the outskirts of our cities. We know the measures we must take to clean the streets and purify the air. The demand to do so grows. We must control the wastes of our society and preserve our wilderness. Our increasing awareness will cause us to band together and start to do what must be done. It is in the very nature of man to protect his home and his land.

The pictorial engravings on the following pages reflect the image of America a hundred years ago. It was a time of wonder

for the landscape artist, so well equipped with academic drawing skills, with the whole of America lying untouched before him. Stephen Foster's melodies paid homage to the rivers and the mountains, and the poets, like Longfellow at Gloucester, caught the spirit of the Atlantic:

> "And fast through the midnight dark and drear,
> Through the whistling sleet and snow,
> Like a sheeted ghost the vessel swept
> Toward the reef of Norman's Woe."

From the Delaware Water Gap came a simpler couplet full of respect for the power of the river:

> "Kittatinny House, that on a rock is founded,
> So, when floods come, the folks won't be drownded."

One contributor to *Picturesque America* wrote: "Descending into the damp, fresh valley, and making your way through the woods, the aromatic odor of a hundred different growing things greets your nostrils. . . . The ride goes on till the great stars quiver in the dark vault of the heavens, that seem the deeper and more mysterious from their framework of mountain peaks."

As America continues to grow and to change, these engravings will be used again and again to measure our progress in art as well as in conservation. We shall never again know the uncomplicated innocence of our small cities, or the sight of the stagecoach thundering across the mountain bridge. Only for a short time longer will we hold the fading memory of children playing on top of a horse-drawn hay rig, and the sound of sleigh bells in a winter night. The responsibility for the future always lies with us. Together we can shape the future of the cities and the destiny of our land. This idea was quaintly, yet accurately, stated in *Picturesque America* a century ago; and so it remains today:

"Blessed be the memory of the fathers, in that they had the good taste to plant these trees, under whose grateful shades their posterity might linger, and whose green foliage might add so much to the beauty of the homes which they were rearing, not for themselves only, but for their children who should come after them."

Arthur A. Houghton, Jr.
President, The Metropolitan Museum of Art
July 1969

The Capitol, from the Botanic Gardens

The capital of the United States rests gracefully beside the Potomac. From Arlington on the Virginia side of the river, one sees the great domed Capitol looming majestically above the surrounding government buildings. If one stands on the rear portico of the President's House, there is a splendid view of the red castlelike Smithsonian Institution and the Washington Monument rising like a slender marble spear. At every step in this beautiful city one sees some reminder of its exciting history, and thinks of the dedicated statesmen who have served the country.

Washington, from Arlington Heights

Mount Desert, Coast of Maine

View from Via Mala, at The Ovens

Mount Desert Island is a place of wild beauty on the rugged coast of Maine. Beside the waves, the rocks are tumbled one upon another in titanic disorder, and the mountains are sheared away in frightful precipices. From these mountains, one has an eagle's view of the farthest reaches of the sea and the coast guarded by a dark green forest of fir and spruce. The bays and inlets offer superb protection for the intrepid yachtsman. The Ovens are great cavities worn in the rock by tides, a famous picnic place abounding with starfish, sea urchins, anemones, and other strange and beautiful forms of sea life. In Maine, they say, even the fog has a certain grace and charm.

*B*oston was once a Pilgrim's wilderness that has been made to blossom like
the rose. A glance from the harbor takes in the whole of the Boston shipping, the
wharves and docks crowded with water craft of every shape and size, the State House
dome with its gilded cupola watching over Beacon Hill, and the stark granite shaft of
Bunker Hill Monument looming over the suburb of Charlestown. In nearby Cambridge
is Harvard University with edifices of various styles used by the scholars. Here are
old brick dormitories, a solid granite anatomical museum, a splendid library and rare
book collections which have been gradually formed for generations.

Harvard College Buildings

City of Boston, from South Boston

On the Beverly Coast, Massachusetts

Swallows' Cave, Nahant

Along the northern shore of Massachusetts Bay, between Boston and Cape Ann, irregular peninsulas with rocky shores and noble beaches jut into the sea. Here one can relish both the cheerful and rugged aspects of marine nature, as the coast affords ample opportunities for fishermen, bathers, and loungers by the sea. Within convenient distance of Boston are spots where a man may deposit his whole family for the summer in a long-porched hotel or build for them a cozy cottage quite within daily access of his business haunts. At Swallows' Cave, Nahant, one may enter for some distance by row boat. It is a cool haunt in the hottest days of summer when the beaches are insufferable.

The Conway Road, near Mount Washington

The regular stagecoach passes among the White Mountains and valleys and the passengers delight in the pungent fragrance that emanates from the resinous woods. The ascent of Mount Washington gives a person really fond of mountain scenery an overwhelming sense of exhilaration. Here and there are springs of most delicious cool mountain water, where the heated horses and riders may stop for a moment to drink. As one emerges upon the summit, the small yet hardy Alpine plants appear among the rocks. Down in the valley lies the Emerald Pool, a sunny basin, bright and still, full of swift trout to tempt the ardent angler.

Emerald Pool, the White Mountains

Connecticut Valley, from Mount Tom

*F*rom its source near the Canadian border, the Connecticut River flows grandly through the whole length of New England. The river valley is the center of a region where future generations plan to live from the products of the fertile soil and the immense water power used to manufacture commercial goods. In the valley beneath Mount Tom, one can see the Oxbow, Northampton, Hadley, South Hadley, Hatfield, Amherst, and north to the Green Mountains in Vermont. The valley of the Connecticut possesses a wonderful beauty of extensive meadows and overshadowing hills. The Indians who first lived here built their camps along the banks of the river. They called Springfield, "Agawam," and Hartford, "Suckiaug."

White River Junction

The Abbott House

In the year 1635, the Massachusetts Bay Company thought it necessary to banish Roger Williams, then a minister at Salem, as his views of religious liberty were regarded as unscriptural and dangerous. He and his associates proceeded to establish a settlement at Providence among the Narragansett Indians. The names of the city's thoroughfares show us the settler's esteem for the cardinal virtues: Benevolent Street, Benefit Street, Faith Street, Happy Street, Hope Street, Joy Street, and others. What is known as the Abbott House is an ancient structure in which Roger Williams is said to have held his prayer meetings. Today almost every thing is manufactured in this great city, and the mills are grand in size.

City of Providence, from Prospect Hill

The broad stretch of Narragansett Bay, which opens directly south of Providence and extends for thirty miles down to the Atlantic, causes people from all parts of the Union to flock here to enjoy the cool ocean air. Perhaps the greatest feature of this place is the clambake, an institution of which Rhode Islanders are rightly proud, and regard as a connecting link that binds them to the old Narragansett Indians with whom it originated. On many a summer evening, clams in the shell are baked upon heated stones under a thick layer of fresh seaweed.

View from the Coast

Indian Rock, Narragansett

The Walk on the Cliff, Newport

The island on which Newport stands was originally called "Aquidneck," or the "Isle of Peace." In colonial days a peaceful liberty of conscience existed here. This encouraged a large population to settle and develop a thriving port. Alas, the Revolutionary War and the embargo of the War of 1812 ruined the commercial aspects of Newport. Now it has become a most fashionable resort. The summer residents of Newport may be seen driving in their splendid carriages, or sailing in their yachts along the Narragansett shores, or resting in their immense "cottages" lining the spacious avenues. In the summer season, recreation includes bathing on the beach and healthful walks along the cliff. It is said that the true purpose of these gatherings is for pleasant talk and chastened conviviality away from the high-strung excitement of American life.

The Drive

New Haven Elms

New Haven is on the Connecticut shore of Long Island Sound. Yale College and the Green stand at the center of the city. East and West Rocks are striking bluffs of traprock rising 400 feet above the elm-lined streets. The cliffs are rough and difficult to climb, but from these summits on a clear day the spectator may stretch his vision across the Sound and see Long Island. Along the shore travelers may enjoy bathing, boating, and the delicious summer breezes.

East Rock, New Haven

The Housatonic

Ice Glen, Stockbridge

The Housatonic River springs from the beautiful Berkshire region of
Massachusetts and flows for a hundred pleasant miles to the south until it empties
into Long Island Sound. Throughout this river valley one is charmed by the
blossoming orchards, crystal lakes, and silvery waterfalls tumbling through the glens.
The soft line of the river stretches amid picturesque homesteads which now and then
cluster into villages. Rustic bridges, white farm houses, and red barns surrounded by
grazing cattle and sheep mingle together to surprise and satisfy the eye.

Montauk Point

At the eastern tip of Long Island lies Montauk Point, a bold solitary arm of land. The storms here are grand to see, as the mighty Atlantic thunders in with unbroken force against the shores, and the wrecks that strew the coast are pitiful reminders of the terrible tragedies of the past. On the extreme point stands a tall white lighthouse, erected in 1795, and one of the best known lights on the coast. The crisp, delicious smell of the salt air from the sea, the sudden mists, and the beaches with the ever tumbling surf, give a feeling of exhilaration and of repose. Nearby are East Hampton, Southampton, Greenport, and Sag Harbor, quiet towns, neat and green.

Moonlight on Shore

The Terrace, Central Park, New York

*A*t the southern tip of New York is the Battery and a pleasure promenade with a fine sea wall. Castle Garden has seen vast bodies of immigrants pass into America as they start life in the New World. Fifth Avenue, the highway of fashion, leads to the beginning of Central Park. The park was planned with extreme care and is the pride of the metropolis. There is a union of art with nature in its splendid museum, its many bridges, its Italian-like terrace, its lakes, its secluded leafy rambles and picturesque nooks. The promenades are unexcelled abroad. The superb drives are thronged with vehicles, and on summer afternoons the paths are occupied by immense numbers of people. There is a menagerie tolerably well filled and performances of gay music. For the children there are goat carriages and camel riding.

The Battery and Castle Garden

Clinton Street, Brooklyn

Directly opposite New York lies Brooklyn, where the air is crisp and bright. It is an attractive city with handsome tree-embowered streets. The Heights command wonderfully stirring views of Manhattan, the bay, and the East River. Mingling here are white-sailed ships, black-funnelled steamers, winged pleasure yachts, snorting tugs, tall-masted schooners, barges, canal boats, and swift ferries. They all move amid the fleets of anchored ships from whose gaffs fly the flags of far-off nations. Where the old tars assemble on the East River wharves, the square-rigged ships discharge their precious cargoes, and merchants of the old Knickerbocker quality conduct their business in dark chambers.

City of New York, from Brooklyn Heights

West Point and the Highlands

The Old Newburgh Toll Road

*O*n a remarkable and beautiful promontory extending into the Hudson River lies West Point, the site of our important military school and one of the most attractive spots in the whole country. Turn in any direction from the parade ground, the recognized central point of the post, and new points of outlook and fresh beauty await everywhere, especially on the wooded shores descending sharply to the water. One should pass along the western shore on the old toll road, as well as make the voyage upon the river, to catch the full beauty of Newburgh at the northern entrance of the Highlands. Newburgh has one of the most perfect harbors of the Hudson, and was Washington's headquarters during a part of the Revolution.

View from Peekskill

Peekskill stands near the southern entrance of the Hudson River Highlands. The town is very picturesque with its houses lying on the sloping lower shore and a terraced road on the steep hillside behind. From this point one may look out on the long, clear reaches of the open river. Nearby are scenes touched by the pen of Washington Irving: Tarrytown, Tappan Zee, and Sleepy Hollow, legendary places haunted by Dutch goblins. The Moodna is one of the many picturesque creeks tumbling into the Hudson River. Throughout this region there is an atmosphere of peace and quiet as if eons of happy years have glided away since man first led cows to graze and sheep to nibble on the rich pastures.

Mouth of the Moodna, on the Hudson

Lake George

Studded in the center of New York state are the loveliest lakes in the world, adorned with beautiful villages romantically situated amid rocky glens. Lake Champlain and Lake George, united by a narrow rivulet, are the most famous historically, forming part of the often contested water route to Canada. Fort Ticonderoga on the southern end of Lake Champlain was first built by the French, then held by the English, and later captured in the Revolution by the American patriot, Ethan Allen, and his Green Mountain Boys. The placid waters and glorious landscapes may be seen from the steamboats that make daily trips, or explored independently with a canoe or sail boat. Camping parties are a special feature of Lake George, and in the summer months they may be seen on almost all of the larger islands.

View from the Lake Steamer

The Hudson, Twenty Miles from Its Source

The Adirondack is a great wilderness of northern New York where lofty mountains tower far above hundreds of scattered lakes. It lies between Lakes George and Champlain on the east, the St. Lawrence on the northwest, and nearly to the Mohawk on the south. The wandering artist and the adventurous hunter camp on leafy river banks where the deer also pasture, wary of the wolf, the panther, and the great black bear. Traveling is done by means of small boats that can be carried on the shoulders from pond to pond. The fare is chiefly trout and venison easily procured by rod and gun; the salmon trout and the speckled trout swarm in the lakes and rivers. Natural curiosities abound in the Adirondack Mountains: the grand black war eagle, owls, loons, ducks, herons, ravens, stake drivers, mud hens, partridges, and kingfishers.

The Adirondack Woods

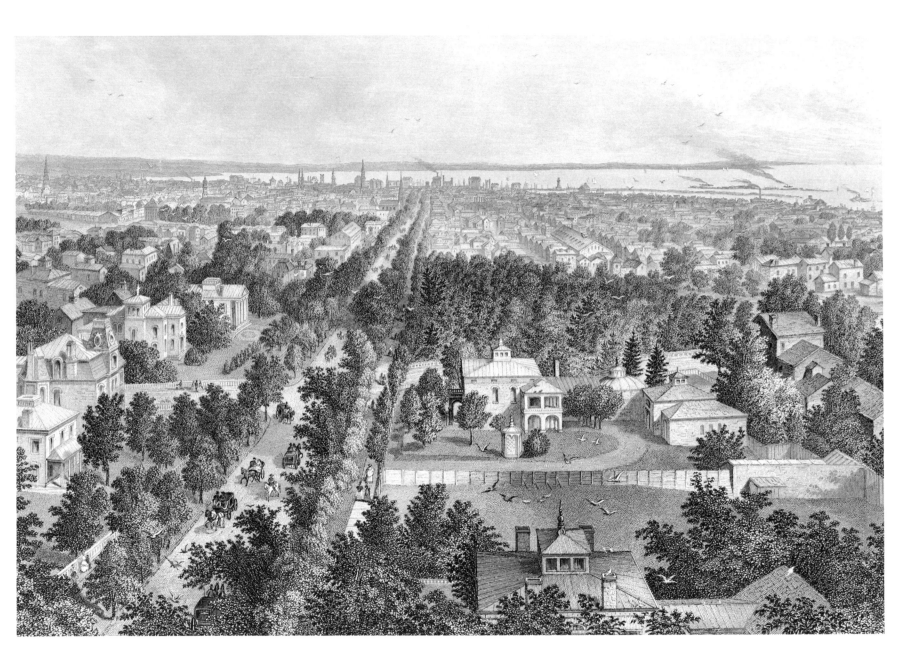

City of Buffalo

At the eastern end of Lake Erie lies the city of Buffalo, named for the American bison that roamed in herds along the shore as late as 1720. Lake Erie derived its name from the Eries, or wildcat Indian tribe, who lived upon its shores when the Jesuit missionaries first visited the country three centuries ago. They were a powerful tribe, but suddenly in 1665 the Iroquois in a single day destroyed them. Only their name lives on. In the town of Erie, Pennsylvania, on the southern shore of the lake, in 1753 the French first built a fort called Presque Isle. The Erie light, with the keeper's little cabin at the base, gleams white by day and red by night, visible for a distance of twenty miles. The lighthouses on the western waters are almost always in view, for the steamers are careful to keep within sight of shore.

Main Light, at Erie

Between the American Falls and the horseshoe shaped Canadian Falls, Goat Island splits the Niagara River as it plunges over the enormous limestone ledges. This magnificent cataract hurls the accumulated waters of the four Great Lakes on their way to the ocean. Here a billowing cloud of smoky spray rises endlessly into the air. The sun shines down upon the seething waters, and its slanting arrows of light are seized by the mist and broken into a thousand hues, into fragmentary rainbows and bubbles of crimson and green. In the winter, when all the vegetation on the islands is incrusted with frozen spray, each tree, each blade of grass is sheathed in a scabbard of diamonds. It is a fearful and fantastic sight.

Tree Crushed by Frozen Spray

Niagara

The Highlands of the Neversink

The wooded heights on the New Jersey coast were named Neversink by the sailors upon the Atlantic who delighted in the fact that the graceful hills remain in view for such a long time. At the foot of the Highlands, near Red Bank, flows the Shrewsbury River, where bass, blue fish, and oysters abound. Beyond the river, Sandy Hook stretches northward to New York's Lower Bay. The railroad runs along the narrow strip of sand that separates the river from the ocean, giving the passengers a charming view of Beacon Hill, crowned by a double-towered lighthouse, the rays of which reach a distance of thirty-five miles, or as far as the altitude of the tower lifts the horizon.

At Red Bank

Bushkill Falls

Near the adjoining boundaries of New York, New Jersey, and Pennsylvania, formed by the Delaware River, there is a mighty gorge cutting through the Kittatinny Mountains. Thought to be too inaccessible for travel by the first Dutch and French settlers in this region, the Gap was long left to the eagles and the rattlesnakes that lived among the frowning cliffs of naked rock. But now there is a serviceable road through it and a railway track skirting the water's edge. Several miles above the Gap, the Delaware is joined by the Bushkill, a mountain stream boasting one of the most beautiful waterfalls of the district, where a swift torrent strikes upon a projecting boulder and rebounds in snowy foam into the dark chamber of rock below.

Delaware Water Gap

Cotton Mills, Ridele's Bank

A little way up the Brandywine at Ridele's Bank the scenery is superb. One lingers in the dense shadows of the river's edge and discovers a strange charm in the mingled sounds of rushing water and buzzing wheels. The hush of leafy woods and the hum of labor seem to blend in delicious harmony, and the gray walls of the mill buildings offer no harsh contrast with the magnificent masses of green forest in which they are placed. Ferns rivaling the choicest pets of the conservatory are found in the mossy ravines, and the scarlet flame of the cardinal flower lights up many a shady retreat. The rapid descent of the Brandywine furnishes the power to the cotton, grist, and gun powder mills for which the city of Wilmington is so justly famous.

Boys Fishing, on the Brandywine

The Schuylkill, from Lansdowne

William Penn planned Philadelphia to be built in the form of a grid consisting of thirty streets crossing each other at right angles between the banks of the Delaware and the Schuylkill. The city, a site of many political and historical events during the American Revolution and early days of our Republic, has grown into a commercial and cultural center far greater than the early Quakers imagined possible. The vast sylvan Fairmont Park, including the famous Fairmont Water Works, was gradually formed by city purchase of some well cultivated estates beside the Schuylkill, including Belmont, once the country home of Judge Peters, a personal friend of General Washington, and the famous Lansdowne estate.

Philadelphia, from Belmont, West Park

The Susquehanna, at Hunter's Gap

The Susquehanna is a river possessed of soft beauties. Flowing from the North and West Branches until it empties into the Chesapeake Bay, it is a joy to behold. Beneath the soil the whole valley is one vast deposit of anthracite coal and in the upper reaches of the river the lumber trade thrives on rich forests. It is no wonder, therefore, that Harrisburg, the political capital of the State of Pennsylvania, is also a thriving manufacturing town. From the cupola of the Capitol one can survey the city tipped with graceful spires and smoking chimneys. The mountains beyond stand tier upon tier, with each range showing a different tinge of blue. The islands in the gleaming Susquehanna are surrounded by shallows filled with broad-leaved rushes that sigh plaintively as the wind passes over them.

Harrisburg, from Brant's Hill

*F*rom the wooded slopes of Druid Hill Park, one has a fine view of the city named after George Calvert, first Lord Baltimore, to whom King Charles I had granted Maryland in 1632. Baltimore lies near the head of Chesapeake Bay, a noted source of excellent terrapin, oysters, and crabs. Fort McHenry is at the entrance of Baltimore harbor. Fort McHenry **gallantly** withstood an attack by the British in September, 1814, and Francis Scott Key, a prisoner on board a ship in the harbor, was so inspired by seeing the besieged flag still flying in the "dawn's early light" after the relentless bombardment that he wrote what became "The Star-Spangled Banner." His verses were first published in the Baltimore Patriot under the title of "The Defense of Fort McHenry."

Fort McHenry

City of Baltimore, from Druid Hill Park

Harper's Ferry by Moonlight

Robert Harper, a native of Oxford, England, was so excited by the beauty of the place where the Potomac and the Shenandoah flow together that in 1747 he bought a tract of land there and established a ferry. Harper's Ferry lies in Jefferson County, West Virginia, just across the Potomac from the Maryland Heights. Having unrivaled water power, it was chosen during the administration of President Washington to be the site of the national armory. On the night of October 16, 1859, John Brown and a small band of men stealthily crossed the railroad bridge from Maryland. Hoping to establish a stronghold in the southern mountains to which slaves could flee, they seized the armory. Robert E. Lee with a force of marines put an end to the raid, but national strife was to follow. During the Civil War the town was often fought over and suffered greatly.

The Maryland Road

The Natural Bridge

Thomas Jefferson delighted in the total beauty of Virginia. When Richmond supplanted Williamsburg as the seat of state government, Jefferson designed the Capitol, placed imposingly on one of the city's many hills. In his Notes on the State of Virginia, published in 1784, Jefferson called the Natural Bridge in the Blue Ridge Mountains the "most sublime of nature's works." From the summit of this terrific stone arch to the stream below, its ancient creator, is 215 feet, 55 feet higher than the falls of Niagara.

Richmond, from Hollywood

65

The Chickahominy

Within the boundaries of Virginia there is a small world of scenic beauties that are infinitely varied. The New River, nestled in a western valley in the Appalachian Mountains, flows peacefully between banks lined with fine sycamores languidly trailing in the water. The Chickahominy in the Tidewater area has both flora common on the rivers of the southern states and also growth of the colder climates. The cypress with its curious roots and funereal moss hanging from its branches grows beside the beech, the maple, and the gum tree. Raccoons, otters, and muskrats roam here and the wood duck with its brilliant plumage flashes over the quiet river like a ray of sunlight.

New River

The Great Smoky Mountains are the highest in the Appalachian range. Their crests form the boundary between Tennessee and North Carolina. The Cherokee Indians called the mountains "Land of the Great Smoke" because of the blue-gray haze often twisting among the towering peaks and rolling into the valleys. "The Suck," thirteen miles below Chattanooga, is a serious obstacle to navigation. This is caused by a fierce little mountain current called "Suck Creek," which in high water strews masses of boulders and debris into the river bed. Boats ascending the river are warped up by means of a windlass on the shore, accompanied by the songs and shouts of the laboring deck hands.

Steamer on the Tennessee

The Great Smoky Mountains

Cumberland Gap

The most celebrated pass through the mountains of eastern Tennessee is Cumberland Gap. Here the mountains rise to 1200 feet, but the Gap is so narrow in places that there is scarcely room for the road, which winds like a huge ribbon around the rocks. This road is the enlarged trail used by Indians, by Daniel Boone, and by homesteaders going west. Through the Blue Ridge Mountains in North Carolina a path is also cut by a river called the French Broad. Old fashioned stagecoaches and country "schooners" drawn by teams of mules lumber over the river road. Cabins are the gathering spots where corn whiskey and mountain news divide the honors of the hour. Pioneers who settled here are proud and intelligent. They are hunters and woodsmen who delight in the wild mountains. They almost live on horseback. Their needs are few, it is said: a gun, a dog, a horse, a cottage, a wife, and a cow—pretty much in that order.

A Team on the French Broad

Bull Street, Savannah

Charleston and Savannah are usually considered to be two of the most handsome cities in America. Both have thriving ports, and in springtime when the trees and shrubbery are in full flower the cities are at their best. In Charleston many beautiful homes were built by wealthy planters, who during the heat of the summer left their cotton and rice plantations to live in the city. Tiers of open verandas and ironwork balconies adorn the ancient structures, and azaleas, camellias, and magnolias, often growing to thrilling heights, color the gardens. In Savannah plazas have been planted with the evergreen and ornamental trees of the old South. Bull Street is the fashionable thoroughfare of Savannah and at all seasons affords delightful, shady walks.

A Garden in Charleston

On the Coast of Florida

The early explorers of Florida hoped to discover gold, but found only an immense sand bar covered with a tropical wilderness. Today we know that this section of the country is remarkable for its recuperative effects, with its warm winters and sulphurous pools. Navigation of the swamps is difficult, but on the Oklawaha River the channel is indicated by blazed marks on the trunks of the towering cypress. The swamps of Florida are rich in birds and vegetation. One of the most attractive birds is the snakebird, that moves its head constantly like a black snake in search of prey. Also, the large white crane proudly stalks about, hunting fish and spearing them with its long, sharp bill. The prominent living object, though, is the alligator, whose paradise is in the swamps and everglades of Florida.

A Sudden Turn on the Oklawaha

St. Francis Street, St. Augustine

St. Augustine was founded by the Spaniards in 1565 and is the oldest European settlement in the United States. This quaint little city with its fort of San Marcos was the scene of many bloody attacks and looting by the French and English for two centuries. Fragrant with the blossoms of the honeysuckle and the acacia, the gardens in the town are well stocked with fruit trees such as figs, guavas, plantains, pomegranates, lemons, limes, citrons, shaddocks, China and Seville oranges, date palms, and grape vines. The island opposite the city at the entrance of the harbor offers an excellent building material in the coquina stone, which becomes hard when exposed to the air and does not splinter when struck by cannon balls. Several buildings in the town are worthy of notice for their charm and antiquity.

A Garden in Florida

City of New Orleans

Planter's House on the Mississippi

When ascending the Mississippi in 1718, Bienville, the first governor of Louisiana, laid the foundations of New Orleans on the first high land he found. Thus founded by the French, the city later was ruled for thirty-eight years by the Spaniards. In 1803 the young United States purchased the city along with the vast Louisiana territory. The broad river opposite New Orleans forms a magnificent bay where steamers, including the "floating palaces" which ply between the cities of the great West, dock beside the ships from every land, making a line of masts and chimneys along the levee embankment. A large number of descendants of the original French settlers live in New Orleans and in the surrounding country where cotton and sugar cane are the main crops of the plantations.

The river banks of the lower Mississippi are referred to as the "coast." There are gardens here upon which the city depends for vegetables and fruit. Rich soil, a warm climate, and abundance of water allow the growth of the choicest tropical plants including the banana. In Louisiana along the bayous and in the swamps are live oaks, tall ghostly cypress, and wonderful flowering magnolias. Spanish moss festooning the trees made a deep and lasting impression on the early French and Spanish explorers. The great streamers, when cured and threshed, leave long black fibers as thick as horsehair which is valuable for the stuffing of mattresses and cushions, and the increasing demand for it opens a new field of enterprise among the denizens of the swamps.

Market Garden on the Coast

The Moss Gatherers

City of Cleveland, from Reservoir Walk

Cleveland was a main town in the possessions of the Connecticut Western Reserve, where many New England emigrants settled in the early days of the 19th century. The territory in this area was granted and regranted again and again and areas of the tracts such as the "Holland Purchase" or the "Black Swamp" are still mentioned. The town lies on both sides of the Cuyahoga River, whose valley now is a dense mass of iron mills, lumberyards, and oil refineries. But all this bustle is hidden away from the town, which stretches above with long avenues and pleasant residences, gardens, velvet lawns, vines, and flowers.

Euclid Avenue, Cleveland

The Ohio, from Marietta

The Allegheny and the Monongahela rivers join at Pittsburgh to form the Ohio, a lovely, gentle river, curving and bending, flowing through the green countryside between North and South. The shallow stern-wheelers travel slowly up and down, and whistle to each other for the channel. If there is a fog at night, the captain ties up his boat to the bank, and all hands go to sleep. Cincinnati is closely built in solid blocks, rising in several plateaus back from the river. There are many fine buildings in Cincinnati, but the true beauty of the city is in its hilly suburbs. Marietta, Ohio, built near a little stockade called Fort Harmar, is the oldest town in the state. Marietta is situated in the picturesque domains of the old New England "Ohio Company," which was organized long ago to check the advance of the French down the river.

City of Cincinnati

City of Detroit, from Canada Shore

The shores of Lake Erie hide the cannon balls and rusting anchors dating from pre-Revolutionary times. Put-in-Bay received its name from Commodore Perry, whose motto was "Don't give up the ship!" During the War of 1812, Perry put in there with his fleet before and after the Battle of Lake Erie, a contest which gained from the British the undisputed control of Lake Erie. Detroit was first a French military trading post used by the courageous voyageurs who carried their trade in goods to the Indian nations of the far West and returned laden with furs. When it was a British post in 1763, the great Ottawa chieftain, Pontiac, attempted to capture it.

Perry's Cave, Put-in-Bay Island

In the straits between Lake Huron and Lake Michigan lies the small picturesque island of Mackinac. For many years the American Fur Company had supply stores and warehouses here and Mackinac was the gayest and busiest post in the chain. Now the town at the foot of the cliff and the fort on the height above show no commercial activity. The business life of the village died out with the fur trade. Here, also, the annual Indian payments were made, when the neighboring tribes assembled by thousands to receive their stipend. The natural scenery of Mackinac is charming. The Arch Rock is a natural bridge 145 feet high and less than three feet wide, spanning the chasm with airy grace. The visitor sits on the cliff's edge and happily breathes in the buoyant air, or rides slowly over the old military roads. The perfume of cedars and juniper alternate with the fresh forest odors of young maples and beeches.

Indian Hut

Arched Rock, Mackinac

Wabash Avenue, Chicago

Chicago and Milwaukee are both on the western shores of Lake Michigan.
Milwaukee is called the "Cream City of the Lakes" because of the yellow bricks used
for building. A large proportion of the population is German, giving the city
distinctive character. There is a giant flour mill, elevators which store millions of
bushels of grain, and immense brick breweries. Chicago lies ninety miles south of
Milwaukee. The destruction by fire in 1871 of the larger part of Chicago was
followed by a rebuilding of the city in a style of splendor that has made it one of the
marvels of the age. Wabash Avenue is of a semi-suburban character, and here at all
fashionable hours may be seen gay throngs of carriages, equestrians, and pedestrians.

City of Milwaukee

Steamboat Rock, Wisconsin River

Rabbits in the Forest

The Wisconsin River flows across the very center of Wisconsin, through backwoods and prairie wastes, until it reaches the Mississippi. A part of the river known as the Dells has six miles of enchanting beauty where the river passes between hills of solid limestone. At one point the rocks rise sharply from the river in imitation of five steamboat sterns moored together. On fine days in summer the water is skimmed by pleasure barges filled with gaily dressed people from neighboring towns. The lumber rafts descending the river are manned by "half savage, outlandish fellows, picturesque in aspect, if nothing else."

Limestone Walls, below St. Paul

The Red River of the North flows slowly through the flat lands of the Dakota Territory and Minnesota. It is a strange river with an evil reputation for its sadness and loneliness. Even the names surrounding it are far from encouraging: Thief River, Snake River, Devil's Lake. The banks of the river are pastoral, and except during the violent spring flooding, the waters are slow and muddy. Occasionally one glimpses an Indian trail through the grass, a tent, and a canoe toiling against the stream. In Minnesota alone, the shallow river is navigable for 400 miles, and is plied regularly by the shallow drafted stern-wheelers. St. Paul, near St. Anthony's Falls, is the end of navigation on the Mississippi. South of the city stand high white limestone walls that echo the sad sound of the locomotives creeping round the great bluffs.

Red River, Dakota

City of St. Louis

Queen's Bluff, below Trempealeau

*S*teamboat pilots consider St. Louis, the Metropolis of the West, the mid-point
between the upper and the lower Mississippi. The older streets are narrow,
dating back to the early settling by the French in 1762, but the new avenues are
wide and lined with elegant mansions. The public works and buildings are beautiful,
and the warehouses handsome. Although railroads compete with steamboats for
freight and passenger traffic, lining the levee are a number of huge steamboats and
smaller ones of shallow draught that ascend the Missouri almost to the mountains.
There are few things in life more agreeable than to sit on the upper deck of a
"floating palace" and watch the panorama of the river. One sees the many limestone
conformations blending with the ever-changing hues of green trees and plains of
grass on the banks, and famous landmarks such as Queen's Bluff and Trempealeau.

97

Red Buttes, Laramie Plains

The brave pioneers who crossed the great plains of America must have experienced a wild feeling of freedom. The chains that bound them to the east were broken and they looked with hope across the vast, fertile plains in the valleys of the Platte and the Missouri. They looked to a promised land, but they had to cross some regions that were barren, unproductive wastes. It is not now surprising to see a human skeleton beside a broken wagon and the bones of horses. Here stand walls of deserted adobe houses where men sat and planned great roads and cities that died in the dust. Hills and buttes break the monotony of the horizon of the plains and are seen grouped together like fantastic fortresses, looking lonely, weird, and strong.

Emigrants Crossing the Plains

Tower Falls

Yellowstone, in the Wyoming Territory, is truly one of the great wonders of the world. Its mountain meadows, wild life, and falling waters make it the vision of a lifetime. It is a tremendous credit to our government that this wondrous natural site has been set aside as a National Park reserved for the American people forever. The park during the months of June, July and August has a climate that is pure and invigorating. There is frost every month of summer and scarcely a drop of rain. The visitor will be amazed at the constant wonders that surround him. The earth rumbles as huge geysers spurt into the clear air. Mud boils, and hot springs vaporize into clouds of steam that drift across the weird rock cliffs. When seeing the crashing beauty of Tower Falls, one thinks humbly of the wonder of the earth's creation.

Hot Springs, Yellowstone

The Rocky Mountains

The Rocky Mountains are sometimes called the great "Snow-Divide" of the continent. Long's and Pike's Peaks, Garden of the Gods, Estes Park, and Mountain of the Holy Cross are but some of the famous places that challenge the mountaineer. Traveling among the rugged ranges, one hears the murmur of a thousand mountain streams and the moaning winds high above the peaks. It is a place of endless wonder and everlasting grandeur. Ascending the perilous heights and peering down into the awful chasms, one can imagine the ice goblins struggling beneath the white fields of virgin snow. The air is sharp and clear in this land of the eagle and the mountain lion, the grizzly and the big horn sheep. There are few frontier settlements in the mountain wilderness, and these are mostly gold and silver mining towns such as Black Hawk and Central City.

Mountain Falls

Mount Hood, the highest peak in Oregon, rises in cold, noble splendor from the forest beside the Columbia River. Captain Robert Gray named the beautiful Columbia River in 1792, and thirteen years later Lewis and Clark explored its bank for the United States government. The lengthy river running along the northern boundary of Oregon has myriad characteristics: tame water, wild cascades, wide open shores, narrow rocky straits, and always the purest of water. Where the river rushes through narrow channels, there are the famous Salmon Falls. Here the fish run, and leap to reach the spawning grounds of the upper river. The salmon flash briefly against the gleaming white rapids, a wonderful natural sight of power and purpose. The Indians catch the fish and smoke dry them for their store of winter food.

Salmon Falls

Mount Hood, from the Columbia

Californians Lassoing a Bear

California is a land of mountains and broad fertile valleys. Even before the Gold Rush, emigrants went there to seek their fortune, traveling overland and in sailing vessels around the Horn. It was a wild, open country where every horseman was a hunter, and a close encounter with a grizzly bear was thought to be merely sport. The Indians there have soft, musical voices. In the mountains, young squaws sometimes surprise the traveler by preparing for their bath without any concern for the distance. Bare as mermaids, they frolic for an hour in the icy waters of the emerald green rivers. The vast shade trees provide for the traveler a haven against the blinding power of the noonday sun.

Yosemite Fall and Merced River

Fallen Sequoia

Yosemite lies among the highest of the Sierra Nevada Mountains of California.
Its peaks, canyons, lakes, streams, waterfalls, and valley meadows possess a
magnificent grandeur. When following the horse trails into the valley, at each angle
the traveler finds rewarding scenery. The majestic El Capitan and Cathedral Rocks
beside Bridalveil Fall form the southern gateway to the park's main valley.
In spring the valley is filled with the sound of roaring water, as the snows melt and
rush down into the clear lakes. In one of the groves of giant sequoias a trail lies
through the hollow section of one of the fallen redwoods, and a man on horseback can
barely touch the timber arch overhead. These ancient trees with towerlike trunks of
huge diameter are wildly beautiful.

Mirror Lake, Yosemite Valley

Mount Shasta

California knows many rough fellows who found their way across the plains:
mule skinners, miners, and peddlers. All of them are handy with a rifle and a knife.
They hover between the borders of civilization and lawlessness. Horse racing
causes great excitement, and these Californians ride bareback, lashing at their Indian
ponies. A watching crowd bursts into shouts, laughter, and amusing profanity.
In the region of Mount Shasta, lake and field, naked crag and towering
pine-clad crest succeed each other with savage grandeur. Mount Shasta is set upon a
broad base that sweeps out far and wide in every direction, rising upward in one
tremendous sweep. The extinct volcanic cone of Shasta rises to well over 14,000
feet, mingling the rich colors of lava with the snow-clad summit.

Horse Racing

Alcatraz Island

From the schooner's deck in the bay at San Francisco one can see the town of Oakland at the far side, for the air is pure and serene. The islands, too, show plainly, including Alcatraz, an impressive rock rising in the middle of the bay. The waters of the mighty Pacific come here to rest. A feeling of peacefulness abounds, quite different from the crashing waves of the raging ocean that borders the continent. A morning haze often envelops this area, wrapping itself tenderly around the many lovely hills of San Francisco.

Oaks of Oakland

To survey all the beauty of the Golden Gate it is necessary to climb Telegraph Hill, elevated above the roofs and buildings of San Francisco. The portals of the "Gate" seem but a mile apart, a majestic frame for the three-masted merchantmen that have traversed the stormy waters around Cape Horn. The Gold Rush once made San Francisco a wild port for adventurers. Today it has become one of America's most beautiful cities.

On the Coast of California

Golden Gate, from Telegraph Hill

ARTISTS

A. F. Bellows
J. W. Casilear
F. O. C. Darley
Harry Fenn
W. H. Gibson
R. Swain Gifford

C. G. Griswold
J. M. Hart
William Hart
A. S. Hazeltine
David Johnson
J. F. Kensett

Homer Martin
Thomas Moran
Granville Perkins
C. Rosenberg
W. L. Sheppard
James D. Smillie

Jules Tavernier
A. C. Warren
Alfred R. Waud
W. Whitteredge
J. D. Woodward

WRITERS

G. W. Bagby
Sallie A. Brock
Henry A. Brown
O. B. Bunce
E. L. Burlingame
J. C. Carpenter
Robert Carter

Susan N. Carter
T. M. Clarke
J. E. Colburn
John Esten Cooke
F. G. de Fontaine
R. E. Garczynski
C. D. Gardette

Rossiter Johnson
W. C. Richards
W. H. Rideing
J. E. Ringwalt
L. J. G. Runkle
James D. Smillie
D. H. Strother

J. R. Thompson
W. V. Thompson
T. B. Thorpe
G. M. Towle
W. S. Ward
W. F. Williams
Constance F. Woolson

ENGRAVERS

E. P. Brandard
G. R. Hall
H. B. Hall
R. Hinshelwood
F. Holl

S. V. Hunt
D. G. Thompson
W. Wellstood
and others